Anonymous

American Rules for Trap Shooting

Adopted by the National gun association, and revised game laws for western states and territories. April 1, 1890

Anonymous

American Rules for Trap Shooting
Adopted by the National gun association, and revised game laws for western states and territories. April 1, 1890

ISBN/EAN: 9783337196837

Printed in Europe, USA, Canada, Australia, Japan

Cover: Foto ©Suzi / pixelio.de

More available books at **www.hansebooks.com**

Gun Club Rules and

REVISED GAME LAWS

WESTERN STATES AND TERRITORIES

Compliments of the Passenger Department

UNION PACIFIC

THE OVERLAND ROUTE

C. S. MELLEN,
Gen'l Traffic Manager,

E. L. LOMAX,
Gen'l Pass. Agent,

OMAHA, NEB.

American Rules for Trap Shooting

ADOPTED BY

THE NATIONAL GUN ASSOCIATION

AND

REVISED

GAME LAWS

FOR

WESTERN STATES AND TERRITORIES.

April 1, 1890.

CAUTION.

The Game Laws printed herein are corrected up to date. Owing to frequent changes being made at the session of each legislature, we would advise sportsmen and hunters to make inquiry from the State or Territorial officials to learn if any changes have been made.

C. S. MELLEN,
Gen'l Traffic Manager,

E. L. LOMAX,
Gen'l Passenger Agent,

OMAHA, NEB.

AMERICAN RULES

FOR TRAP SHOOTING.

Adopted by the National Gun Association.

ART. I.—REFEREE AND JUDGES.

RULE 1. *Decision of Judges.*—Before the commencement of any match, two impartial judges shall be selected by a majority vote of the contestants, and these two shall select a referee. The judges shall, if possible, decide all questions arising during the match. They shall decide by agreeing within five minutes, or it shall be considered to be a disagreement, and thereupon the referee shall act.

RULE 2. *Decision of Referee.*—The referee shall act only in case of a disagreement of the judges, and his decision shall be absolutely final. No person shall make any remarks calculated to influence the judges or referee while the shot is under decision.

RULE 3. *Exclusive Duties of Referee.*—The referee shall have exclusively the following duties:—

A. He shall see that the traps are properly set before and kept in proper setting during the match. He shall endeavor to make the birds conform to the flight and direction indicated in Article III of these rules.

B. He shall test any trap upon application of a shooter, at any time, by throwing a trial bird therefrom.

C. He shall select one cartridge from those of the shooter at the score, and publicly test the same for proper loading.

D. If a bird thrown is to be declared "no bird," he shall declare it such before the shot is taken, if possible; even if so declared, it shall be scored if accepted, whether hit or missed.

E. He shall see that each shooter, before shooting, is provided with the cards specified herein, and has complied with all the rules which qualify him to shoot.

F. He shall see that no person whatever shall stand, while the shooter is at the score, within a radius of fifteen feet from the score, the puller, scorer, judges, or referee.

G. He shall see that no challenges are allowed, except made by contesting shooters.

H. He may, in his discretion, refuse to permit a shooter to continue shooting in a round, who has not come to the score within three minutes after being called thereto by the scorer.

ART. II.—THE SCORE AND SCORING.

RULE 4. *Order of Shooting.*—In individual sweepstakes or matches, shooters shall be called to the score in the order as successively entered. When the number of birds is seven singles or under, each shooter will remain at the score until he has finished the same; when the number exceeds 7 singles, each shooter shall successively fire a score of 5 singles, and, when all have done likewise, will duly repeat same until the score is finished.

When the number of birds combines "so many singles" and "so many doubles," the shooters shall first finish the "singles" as per the foregoing rule, and shall then finish the "doubles" in like manner, viz., each shooter firing at 5 pairs doubles, and then retiring, etc., etc.

RULE 5. *Flags for Judges.*—Each judge shall be provided with a red flag and a white flag or guidon. They shall raise the red flag to indicate a broken or killed bird, and the white flag to indicate "lost bird;" they shall raise both flags to indicate "no bird" or an "imperfect bird." The judges and scorer shall also promptly announce the score in a loud tone of voice.

RULE 6. *Use of Second Barrel.*—Where special matches are arranged, allowing the use of both barrels at single birds, a kill or break with the second barrel shall be scored one-half.

RULE 7. *Scoring Incorrect Handicap.*—No member is to shoot at a distance nearer than that at which he is handicapped. If he does so, the first time the shot shall be scored "no bird;" the second time it shall be scored a "lost bird;" and the third time he shall forfeit all rights in the contest, and be barred from all other contests during the same meeting, and be subject to such additional fines and penalties as the Constitution and By-Laws may provide.

RULE 8. *Closing of Entries.*—All entries shall close at the firing of the first gun. In large international or interstate tournaments, all entries for the first match each day shall be made before 6 P. M. of the day preceding the shoot, by depositing 10 per cent of the entrance fee, which shall be forfeited to the management if the entry is not completed before the firing of the first gun.

RULE 9. *Class Shooting.*—All sweepstakes shall be Class Shooting unless otherwise specified.

RULE 10. *Names Claimed.*—The Secretary shall keep a book in which he shall record the names of all the members who desire to shoot under an assumed name, and record the name assumed by each. He shall make a charge of 50 cents, and no more, for each name recorded. No two members shall shoot under the same assumed name. The Secretary may, at the request of a member, issue the handicap card to him, bearing his assumed title only.

RULE 11. *Score with Ink only.*—All scoring shall be done with ink or indelible pencil. The scoring of a "lost bird" shall be indicated by a "0;" of a "dead" or "broken" bird by a "1."

ART. III.—THE TRAPS.

RULE 12. *Arrangement of Traps.*—Five traps shall be used. They shall be set level upon the ground, without any inequalities of setting in either, in an arc of a circle, five yards apart. The radius of the circle shall be 18 yards. The traps shall be numbered from No. 1, upon the left, to No. 5, upon the right, consecutively. In all traps, except No. 3, the fourth notch, or a maximum velocity equivalent thereto, shall be used, and the elevation of the projecting arm shall not exceed 15 degrees, viz., so as to throw the pigeons from four to fifteen feet in vertical height above the level of the trap bottom. In trap No. 3, the third notch, or a velocity equivalent thereto, shall be used, with the same elevation.

RULE 13. *Setting of Traps.*—A straight line shall be drawn from the score, at eighteen yards in the rear, to trap No. 3, and extended to a point not further than seven yards in front of same. Traps Nos. 1 and 5 shall be set to throw the birds across this line, the crossing point being anywhere within the seven yards point in front of trap 3. Trap No. 2 shall throw in a direction left half quartering from the score; trap No. 4 shall throw in a direction right half quartering upon the score; and trap No. 3 shall throw straight-away.

If, after such setting of the traps, the birds, for any reason, take other directions, they shall be considered fair birds.

RULE 14. *Pulling of Traps.*—When the shooter calls "Pull" the trap shall be instantly sprung, or the bird may be refused. If pulled without notice, or more than one bird loosed, the shot may be refused; but, if taken it is to be scored. If the shooter fails to shoot when the trap is properly pulled, it must be scored a lost bird.

RULE 15. *Position of Puller.*—The trap-puller shall stand from four to six feet behind the shooter, and shall use his own discretion in regard to which trap shall be sprung for each shooter, but he shall pull equally and regularly for all shooters.

RULE 16. *Screens, Netting, Trench.*—No screens or netting shall be used; "back stops" may be provided for trappers not to exceed ten yards from the end traps, and not to exceed three feet in height.

But, when the grounds permit, a trench may be dug to shield the trapper, without obstructing the view of the traps from the shooter.

RULE 17. *Double Birds, Trap Setting.*—Doubles shall be thrown from traps Nos. 2 and 3.

Trap No. 3 shall be set at about fifteen degrees elevation; trap No. 2 at about twenty degrees elevation, in double bird shooting; and trap No. 4, when used for shooting off ties in doubles, shall be set at about the latter elevation.

RULE 18. *Ties and Traps for Ties.*—Ties on single birds shall be thrown from traps Nos. 1, 2, and 5.

Ties on double birds from traps Nos. 3 and 4.

ART. IV.—THE GUN.

RULE 19. *Position of Gun.*—The gun shall be held below the arm-pit. until the shooter calls "Pull;" otherwise, if challenged, the shot shall be declared a "lost" bird, whether hit or missed.

RULE 20. *Loading of Gun.*—Charge of powder unlimited; charge of shot not to exceed 1¼ oz., Dixon's standard measure, No. 1106 "dipped" measure. Any shooter using a larger quantity of shot shall forfeit all entrance money and rights in the match, and shall be subject to further action by the management, as provided in the Constitution and By-Laws.

RULE 21. *Handicap of Gun.*—No guns larger than 10 bore shall be allowed. Guns of 12 gauge weighing 8 pounds or under, shall be allowed two yards. Guns of smaller calibre than 12 gauge shall be shot at the same rise as the latter.

ART. V.—The Inanimate Target or Clay Pigeon.

RULE 22. *Broken Birds.*—No clay pigeon shall be retrieved to be examined for shot marks. A clay pigeon, to be scored broken, must be broken so as to be plainly seen in the air; that is a piece must be clearly and perceptibly broken from it in the air by the shot, before it touches the ground.

RULE 23. *Lost Birds.*—A. All clay pigeons not broken in the air as above defined, and not ruled as "no birds," shall be scored lost.

B. When shooting at single clay pigeons, one barrel only shall be loaded; should more than one barrel be loaded, the shot shall be scored lost.

RULE 24. *Imperfect or "No Birds."*—If a clay pigeon be broken by the trap, it shall be optional with the shooter to accept it; if he accepts, the result shall be scored.

RULE 25. *Allowing Another Bird.*—The shooter shall be allowed another clay pigeon under either of the following contingencies:—

A. In single bird shooting, if two or more are sprung instead of one.

B. If the pigeon is sprung before or at any noticeable interval after the shooter calls "Pull."

C. If the pigeon does not fly 28 yards from its trap, passing over a line (imaginary), at a distance of 10 yards from the traps, and 4 feet high at the latter distance. The spirit of this rule is to this effect: that the bird shall attain an elevation of not less than 4 feet within 10 yards from the trap.

D. If the shooter's gun, being properly loaded and cocked, does not go off through any cause whatever, except through the fault of the shooter.

E. If a pigeon is thrown so that to shoot in proper time it would endanger life or property.

But if the shooter, in either of the foregoing contingencies, fires at the pigeon, he is to be deemed as accepting it, and the shot must be scored according to its results.

RULE 26. *Double Birds.*—A. In case one be a fair bird and the other an imperfect or no bird, the shooter shall shoot at a new pair; both birds must be sprung at once, otherwise they shall be "no birds."

B. If a shooter fires both barrels at one bird in succession, they shall be scored lost.

C. In double bird shooting, in case of misfire of either barrel, through no fault of the shooter, he shall shoot at another pair.

ART. VI.—RISES AND TIES.

RULE 27. *The Rise.*—The rise, in championship matches and sweepstakes, where no handicap has been recorded, when 10 bore guns are used, shall be eighteen yards in single, and fifteen yards for double clay pigeon shooting. When ties are shot off, the rise shall be increased two yards until the limit of the handicap is reached. See handicap rules.

RULE 28. *Ties.*—Ties shall be shot at singles at three birds each, and at doubles at one pair.

Ties in championship matches shall be shot at five singles (thrown from five traps) and two doubles.

RULE 29. *Time of Shooting Ties.*—All ties shall be shot off on the same grounds, immediately after the match, if they can be concluded before sunset. If they can not, they shall be concluded on the following day, unless otherwise directed by the judges. This, however, shall not prevent the ties from dividing the prizes by agreement. Should one refuse then the tie must be shot off. Any one of the persons tieing, being absent thirty minutes after the time agreed upon to shoot them off, without permission of the judges, shall forfeit his right to shoot in the tie.

RULE 30. *Extreme Limit Tie.*—When a shooter is to shoot off a tie, who has previously thereto been handicapped to the extreme limit, he and his opponents shall shoot in the tie at the same distance they each occupied when it occurred.

ART. VII.—TEAM SHOOTING.

RULE 31. *What Constitutes a Club.*—The only club which will be recognized by the Association for the purpose of contests, is a club which has been duly organized, with the usual officers, and a *bona-fide* membership of permanent standing, which maintains its organization by stated meetings and practical work. No clubs can be extemporized and admitted solely for the purpose of shooting in contests.

RULE 32. *Age of Clubs and Members.*—Clubs entering teams must be known as regularly organized gun clubs at least one month previous to the tournament; members of entered teams must be in good standing the same length of time, and be endorsed by the President and Secretary of their respective clubs. Shooters belonging to two or more clubs must shoot with their home clubs, and can shoot with one team only.

RULE 33. *Order of Shooting.*—The teams, in team shoots, will be called to the "score" in the order designated by the Executive Committee; said order will be determined by the dates of original entry, teams being allowed to choose accordingly: the members of the team will be called to the "score" in the order designated by their respective captains, each number shooting at five single birds in succession, and then (when all the teams have finished shooting at single birds) the members will, in a similar manner, finish their scores at the double birds.

RULE 34. *What Constitutes a Team.*—In team championship matches, teams of three to five must be residents of the same State, and in twin team championship matches, both must be residents of the same county or parish. Any State or county can enter as many teams as they see fit. In team or club match other than championships, there shall be no restrictions as to residence of members excepting as stated in the program.

RULE 35. *No Division of First Championship Prize.*—In all championship matches, whether teams or individuals, there shall be no division of prizes or purses among the first scorers or winners of first championship prizes, money or badges, under penalty of expulsion from the Association.

ART. VIII.—PURSES.

RULE 36. *Division of Purses.*—In sweepstake matches, if the number of entries is less than twelve, the net purses shall be divided in two sums, viz., 60 per cent and 40 per cent; and if the number of entries is over twelve and less than forty, the net purses shall be divided into three sums, viz., 50 per cent, 30 per cent, and 20 per cent. If the number exceeds forty, the net purses shall be divided into four sums, viz., 40 per cent, 30 per cent, 20 per cent, and 10 per cent.

RULE 37. *Association Percentage.*—In all tournaments conducted by the Association, five per cent shall be first deducted from all purses for the benefit of the Association; clubs shall deduct two per cent, in club matches, should the club so elect.

RULE 38. *Paying for Birds.*—The price of birds shall be extra, excepting in miss-and-out matches, where it shall be deducted from the entrance purse.

AMERICAN RULES. 7

RULE 39. *Guaranteed Purse.*—Where a purse is guaranteed by the Association, if the entrance fees collectively exceed the guaranteed purse, all such excess shall accrue to the guarantors, viz., the Association; if less, then the Association shall supply the deficiency. Purses mentioned in the program are not guaranteed, unless especially so stated.

ART. IX.—HANDICAPS.

RULE 40. *No Handicaps for Championships.*—In championship contests there shall be no handicap, except for guns; nor shall winners of such contests in team championships be handicapped on account of such winning.

RULE 41. *Permanent Handicap.*—There shall be a Permanent Handicap for each shooter in all other than in championship matches. This handicap shall be made by the Executive Committee, who, immediately after each international or interstate tournament, shall classify every participant therein, and assign to him a handicap which may range from fifteen up to, but not exceed, twenty yards, for singles, and three yards less for doubles. Such handicap shall attach to such shooter thereafter (until altered) in every tournament and match in which he shall engage, when he is shooting in any association sweepstakes; and he must daily begin his shooting at this handicap.

RULE 42. *Temporary Handicap.*—In addition to the permanent handicap there shall be a temporary daily handicap, as follows: If a shooter, having already a Permanent Handicap, shall become a winner in a daily shoot, he shall be handicapped because of such winning, in accordance with the following rule: All winners or dividers of first money shall be handicapped two yards; winners (or dividers) of second money shall be handicapped one yard; maximum handicap, 22 yards. That is to say, if by the scorer's card it appears he is a winner or divider of first money, he shall be handicapped two yards, and of second money, one yard. Winners of third money are not to be handicapped for such winning. Upon presenting the scorer's card, which entitles the shooter to payment of his winnings, the executive officer shall, when paying, mark upon the shooter's handicap card the temporary handicap thus made, which shall govern for the remainder of that day. Provided, however, that in no event shall the maximum of the permanent and temporary handicaps combined exceed 22 yards for "singles," and 3 yards less for "doubles." If the shooter still continues to win at his maximum handicap, the other shooters shall step in towards the traps, the same distance that the successful shooter would otherwise have been placed back.

RULE 43. *New Members' Handicap.*—New members, whose shooting is unknown, shall be handicapped for the first time indicated in Rules 21 and 27, though the Chief Executive Officer shall be authorized to change same, at any time during the tournament, after his present match.

RULE 44. *Non-Winners' Match Handicap.*—Winners in sweepstake matches which are open only to non-winners in previous program matches, shall not be handicapped on account of said winnings in the future program matches of the same tournament, but said winners shall be handicapped in all extra matches, whether shot at the main five traps, or at any extra traps which may be in use on the grounds.

RULE 45. *Extra Match Handicap.*—All matches duly announced in the program are termed "Program Matches;" all others "Extra Matches," whether shot at the main five traps, or at any other traps in use on the grounds. Winners in all "Extra Matches" shall be handicapped according to the above rules in all subsequent extra matches only.

ART. X.—CARDS.

RULE 46. *Handicap Cards.*—The Secretary of the Association shall issue to each member a Handicap Card, which shall bear on its face the name of the shooter, the date of issue, and his permanent handicap, and blanks for temporary handicap records and payment of annual dues. The Secretary shall keep a record of all such cards issued. In the absence of the Secretary, the Chief Executive Officer of the Association on the grounds of a shoot, shall issue such card to any member who has not obtained one, and make a duplicate thereof, to be forwarded to the Secretary.

If the permanent handicap is changed by the Executive Committee, the old card shall be surrendered at the time of issuing the new one.

A permanent handicap shall not be changed during a shooting contest.

When a shooter is called to the score, he shall show his Handicap Card to the scorer (who will mark the handicap on the score book), and also to the referee.

Shooters must provide themselves with Handicap Cards before going to the score.

The Chief Executive Officer shall countersign all Handicap Cards issued by the Secretary. At the beginning of a tournament, shooters shall present their cards to the Executive Officer to be countersigned.

RULE 47. *Pigeon Cards.*—The Secretary shall provide the Chief Executive Officer with "Pigeon Cards," which for live pigeons, shall bear the numbers from 1 to 20 inclusive, and shall be sold by the executive officer for $5; and which, for clay pigeons or other artificial targets, shall be numbered from 1 to 33 inclusive, and shall be sold for $1.50. The same shall bear the signature of the Secretary and the Chief Executive Officer. The scorer will punch these before the pigeons are used. All shooters must provide themselves with the respective cards before going to the score, and unused portions thereof will be redeemed at the rate at which they were issued.

RULE 48. *Winners' Cards.*—At the conclusion of each match, the scorer shall announce the winners, and shall fill out a card containing date, place, and number of the match, name of the winner, whether 1st, 2d, or 3d, etc., number of entries, amount of entrance fee, percentage to be deducted, and sign it as scorer. The winner shall present it to the Executive Officer, who after adding the Temporary Handicap to his record card, shall thereupon pay the amount stated, and make a record of it in his minute book. Any complaint as to the amount stated must be made before receiving payment. These cards must subsequently be transmitted by the Executive Officer to the Secretary.

ART. XI.—PROHIBITIONS AND FINES.

RULE 49. *Prohibitions.*—None but members shall shoot in any contest, unless otherwise announced in the special rules by the Executive Committee.

RULE 50. *Wire Cartridges Prohibited.*—Wire cartridges and concentrators are, on the ground of safety, strictly prohibited; also the admixture of dust, grease, oil, or any other substance to the shot.

RULE 51. *Muzzle-Loaders Prohibited.*—On the ground of safety, and for the general convenience of the shooters, muzzle loaders are prohibited.

RULE 52. *Fines.*—A fine of one dollar, to be added to the purses, shall be rigidly exacted for any of the following acts of negligence:—

A. Pointing a gun at any one under any circumstances.

B. Firing off a gun, except when the shooter has been called to shoot, and is at the score.

C. Closing a gun with cartridge in before arriving at the score, or pointing toward the shooter or spectators when in the act of closing it.

D. Quitting the score without extracting a loaded cartridge unfired.

E. Having a loaded gun anywhere on the ground, except when at the score.

RULE 53. *Fines for Boisterous Wrangling.*—Should any contestant attempt to take any undue advantage of a shooter when at the score, in order to cause him to lose a bird, or should any contestant create or participate in any disturbance, or loud, boisterous wrangling during a shoot, he shall be fined not less than $5, or expelled from the Association, in the manner provided for in the Constitution and By-Laws.

RULE 54. *Bribery.*—Any shooter convicted of an attempt to bribe, or in any manner influence the trappers, judges, scorers, referee or pullers, shall be barred from all further contests during the tournament, and shall be expelled from the Association.

ART. XII.—EXECUTIVE COMMITTEE.

RULE 55. *Changing Sweepstakes.*—Through the Chief Executive Officer, the Executive Committee reserve the right to add to, change, or omit, any sweepstakes or matches.

RULE 56. *Barring Professional Shooters.*—They reserve the right to bar out upon request of any two amateur shooters in the match, any publicly known professional shooter, and also any shooter, who is well known to them to be ungentlemanly or disputatious.

RULE 57. *Recognize No Bets.*—They will not recognize bets, nor decide any matters arising from them. Neither shall judges or referees do so.

RULE 58. *Changing Rules.*—Rules announced to govern tournament shall not be changed within thirty days of the date of the tournament; but while a tournament is progressing, rules may be made to govern future tournaments.

RULE 59. *Duties of Chief Executive Officer.*—All entrance moneys shall be held by the chief executive officer representing the Association on the grounds. He shall divide the purses, retaining the percentages. He shall mark with ink on the handicap card of the winners the date and the temporary handicap for the day, and shall make a record thereof in his daily minute book.

He shall take charge of the score books every night during the tournament.

He shall have authority to employ such subordinates as he may require.

He shall countersign the handicap cards. He shall have authority to change the permanent handicap cards of unknown members.

He shall sell the "Pigeon Cards" and redeem any unused parts thereof.

ART. XIII.—MATCHES PER TELEGRAPH.

RULE 60. Teams or individuals may arrange matches, or the Association may arrange same, to be shot by each at their own respective localities, without coming together, upon complying with the following conditions, viz:—

The entrance fee shall be sent by mail, to the Secretary of the Association, to reach him before the shooting begins. If the entrance fee is not sent by mail, it may be sent by telegraph one hour before the shooting begins. Any person not a member, who desires to enter, may send by mail or telegraph one hour before the shooting begins, an initiation or member's fee of $5, and the entrance fee besides.

All the rules heretofore stated shall apply equally to such matches. Members shall shoot at their permanent handicaps. Those who have no handicap record, shall shoot at the usual distance, 18 yards, etc. The result of each score must be telegraphed as the same is made, to the Secretary of the Association. The scores must also be mailed to him the same day, and their accuracy certified to by the President and Secretary of the local club, or by two disinterested and responsible witnesses who saw the shooting, and who are members of the Association.

Ties shall be shot off, under these rules, upon the twentieth week day thereafter.

The Executive Committee of the Association will duly announce the result, and decide upon any controverted points. The committee shall have full power to make inquiry as to the accuracy of the scores as reported, and to award the money according as the facts may appear.

ART. XIV.—THE LIVE PIGEON.

The following rules (in addition to and modification of the preceding rules), apply to live pigeon matches only:—

RULE 61. *The Traps, Rise, Boundary, Challenged Birds.*—All live birds shall be shot from ground traps, which shall be set five yards apart. Rise 25 yards. Use of one barrel only. Boundary unlimited. In case of challenged bird the shooter allowed three minutes to gather it.

RULE 62. *Birds on the Wing.*—In double bird shooting, the bird shall be on the wing when shot at. A bird shot on the ground shall be scored lost. Double birds to be shot at 21 yards rise, boundary unlimited; five minutes allowed to gather birds if challenged.

RULE 63. *Ties.*—On single birds, 25 yards rise; doubles, at 21 yards rise.

RULE 64. *Lost Birds, No Bird.*—If a bird is shot at, by any person other than the shooter at the score, the referee shall decide whether it shall be scored lost, or whether he will allow another bird. When traps are sprung, should a bird refuse to fly after a reasonable time, the shooter may call "no bird."

RULE 65. *Gathering Birds.*—It shall be optional with the shooter to gather his own birds or appoint a person to do so for him. In all cases the birds must be gathered by hand, without any forcible means, within three minutes from the time it alights, or it shall be scored a lost bird. All live birds must show some shot marks if challenged.

"NEW PERFECTION"
HARDWOOD
HOUSEHOLD REFRIGERATORS.

CHARCOAL

FILLED.

DOUBLE

DOORS.

SUPERIOR TO ALL OTHERS.

IT IS FREE from commingled odors formed in other Refrigerators, and is the only one that produces a pure, dry, cold air, and is more economical in the use of ice than any other Refrigerator made. The ice chamber being large, the consumer can economize by using large cakes of ice, from which much better results are derived.

No moisture will collect upon the walls of the Refrigerator. Matches have been kept in the PROVISION CHAMBERS for weeks and then ignited by striking them upon the zinc in the ICE RESERVOIR, while the "New Perfection" was in constant use and the RESERVOIR well filled with ice all the time, showing that every part of the Refrigerator was dry within.

Messrs. Hibbard, Spencer & Co., the largest Hardware Dealers in Chicago, in speaking of the "New Perfection" Hardwood Refrigerators say: "It needs no comment or praise from us. It is not merely "equal to any in the market, but is positively THE BEST REFRIG- "ERATOR manufactured in the United States."

FOR SALE BY ALL LEADING DEALERS.
BELDING MANFG. CO., MANUFACTURERS,
CHICAGO OFFICE, 185-187 Fifth Ave.

REVISED GAME LAWS

For Western States and Territories.

Game and Fish Laws of Arizona.

PRESERVATION OF GAME AND FISH.—§ 993. It shall not be lawful for any person or persons to take, kill or destroy any **Elk, Deer, Antelope, Mountain Sheep, Mountain Goat** or **Ibex**, in the territory of Arizona, at any time between the first day of February and the first day of October in each year.

§ 994. It shall not be lawful for any person to buy, sell, or have in his or her possession, any of the game animals enumerated in the preceding section, within the time the taking or killing thereof is prohibited, except such as are tamed or kept for show or curiosity.

§ 995. It shall be unlawful for any person to take or catch any fish in any stream, lake or river, pond or pool in the Territory of Arizona with any seine or net.

§ 996. It shall be unlawful for any person in the Territory of Arizona, to shoot or kill any **Partridge, Wild Turkey, Goose, Brant, Swan, Curlew, Plover, Snipe, Rail** or **Ducks**, of any kind, between the first day of March and the first day of September of each year, except on his own premises. And it shall be unlawful for any person or persons, at any time, to trap or net any **Quail, Partridge, Wild Turkey, Grouse, Prairie Chicken**, in this territory, except on his own premises.

§ 997. It shall be unlawful for any person or persons in the Territory of Arizona, to buy, sell or have in his or her possession any of the game birds named in the preceding section, within the time the killing or shooting thereof is prohibited, except such thereof as may be tamed or kept for show or curiosity.

§ 998. It shall be unlawful for any person or persons, at any time, to take, kill or destroy any fish with giant powder, or any other explosive substance.

§ 996. It shall be unlawful for any person or persons, at any time within five years after the passage of this act, to shoot or kill any **Grouse** or **Prairie Chickens** in the Territory of Arizona.

§ 1000. Any person violating any of the provisions of this Title is guilty of a misdemeanor, and shall be fined in a sum not exceeding one hundred dollars, nor less than fifteen dollars, and the costs of prosecution, and in case such fine is not paid, the person or persons so convicted shall be imprisoned in the county jail until said fine is paid; *provided*, such imprisonment shall not exceed one day for each dollar of such fine. Revised Stat., Title 16.

Game and Fish Laws of California.

§ 626. Every person who, in the State of California, between the 1st day of March and the 10th day of September, in each year, hunts, pursues, takes, kills, or destroys any **Quail, Partridge**, or **Grouse**, or **Rail**, is guilty of a misdemeanor. Every person who, in any of the counties of this State, at any time, takes, gathers, or destroys the eggs of any quail, partridge, or grouse is guilty of a misdemeanor. Every person who, in this State, between the 1st day of January and the 1st day of June in each year, hunts, pursues, takes, kills, or destroys **Doves** is guilty of a misdemeanor. Every person who, between the 15th day of December in each year and the 1st day of July in the following year, hunts, pursues, takes, kills, or destroys any **Male Antelope, Deer**, or **Buck** is guilty of a misdemeanor. Every person in the State of California who has in possession any **Hides** of deer, elk, antelope, or mountain sheep killed between the 15th day of December and the 1st day of July is guilty of a misdemeanor. Every person who shall at any time in the State of California, hunt, pursue, take, kill or destroy any **Female Antelope, Elk, Mountain Sheep, Female Deer**, or **Doe**, is guilty of a misdemeanor. Every person who shall at any time hunt, pursue, take, kill, or destroy any **Spotted Fawn** is guilty of a misdemeanor. Every person who shall take, kill or destroy any of the animals mentioned in this section, at any time unless the carcase of such animals is used or preserved by the person slaying it, or is sold for food, is guilty of a misdemeanor. Every person who shall **Buy, Sell, Offer**, or **Expose for Sale, Transport**, or **Have in Possession** any deer, or deer skin, or hide from which evidence of sex has been removed, or any of the aforesaid game at a time when it is unlawful to kill the same provided by this and subsequent sections, is guilty of a misdemeanor. The board of supervisors of the several counties of this State are authorized by ordinance, duly passed and published, to change the beginning or ending of the close seasons named in section 626 of this Code, so as to make the same conform to the needs of their respective counties, whenever, in their judgment, they deem the same advisable. —[Chap. 185, laws 1887.

§ 630. Every person who, in the counties of **Santa Clara, Contra Costa, San Joaquin, Santa Cruz**, or **San Mateo**, uses or distributes phosphorous upon any land or ground between the 1st day of March and the 1st day of November is guilty of a misdemeanor.....§ 631. Every person who shall at any time, net or pound any **Quail, Partridge**, or **Grouse**, and every person who shall sell, buy, transport or give away, or offer or expose for sale, or have in possession, any quail, partridge, or grouse that has been snared, captured, or taken in, or by means of any net or pound is guilty of a misdemeanor. Proof of possession of any quail, partridge, or grouse which shall not show evidence of having been taken by means other than a net or pound, shall be *prima facie* evidence in any prosecution for a violation of the provisions of this section that the person in whose possession such quail, partridge, or grouse is found, took, killed, or destroyed the same by means of a net or pound....§ 632. Every person who, in the State of California, at any time takes or catches any **Trout**, except with hook and line, is guilty of a misdemeanor. Any person who shall, at any time, take, procure, or destroy any fish by means of explosives, is guilty of a misdemeanor....§ 633. Every person who shall take any **Speckled Trout, Brook** or **Salmon Trout**, or any variety of trout, between the 1st day of November and the 1st day of April in the following year, is guilty of a misdemeanor....§ 634. Every person who, between the 31st day of August and the 1st day of October of each year, takes, catches, buys, sells, or has in possession any **Fresh Salmon** or **Shad**, is guilty of a misdemeanor. Every person who shall set or draw, or assist in setting or drawing, any net or seine, for the purpose of taking or catching salmon or shad in any of the public waters of this State, at any time between sunrise on each Saturday and sunset of the following Sunday is guilty of a misdemeanor. Every person who shall, for the purpose of catching salmon or shad, in any public waters of this State, fish with or use any seine or net the meshes [of which] when drawn closely together and measured inside the knot less than seven and one-half inches in length, is guilty of a misdemeanor, and upon conviction shall be fined not less than $100, or in default, not less than one hundred days imprisonment. One-half of all moneys collected for violations go to the informer. But nothing herein prevents the United States fish commissioners or the fish commissioners of the State from taking such fish as they deem necessary for the purpose of artificial hatching at all times....§ 635. Every person who puts into the waters of this State, or uses any **Poisons** or **Explosive Substances** for the purpose of taking or destroying fish is guilty of a misdemeanor....§ 636. Every person who shall set, use or continue, or who shall assist in setting, using, or continuing, any **Pound, Weir, Set Net, Trap**, or any other **Fixed** or **Permanent Contrivance** for catching fish in the waters of this State is guilty of a misdemeanor. Every person who shall cast, extend, or set, any **Seine** or **Net** of any kind, for the purpose of catching fish in any river, stream, or slough, of this State, which shall extend more than one-third across the width of said river, stream, or slough, at the time and place of such fishing is guilty of a misdemeanor. Every person who shall cast, extend, set, use, or continue, or who shall assist in casting, extending, using, or continuing "Chinese sturgeon lines," or "Chinese shrimp or bag nets," or lines or nets of a similar character, for the catching of fish in the waters of this State, is guilty of a misdemeanor. Every person who, by seine or any other means, shall catch the **Young Fish** of any species, which at the time of capture are too small to be marketed, and who shall not return the same to the water immediately and alive, or who shall sell, or offer for sale, any such fish, fresh or dried, is guilty of a misdemeanor. Every person convicted of a violation of any of the provisions of this chapter shall be fined not less than $50 nor more than $300, or be imprisoned not less than thirty days nor more than six months, or both. One-third of all moneys collected for violation of provisions of this chapter shall be paid the informer. It is unlawful to buy or sell, offer or expose for sale, within this State, any kind of Trout (unless brook trout) Less than Eight Inches in Length. Any person violating the provisions of this section is guilty of a misdemeanor....§ 637. Every owner of a dam or other obstruction in the waters of this State who, after being requested by the fish commissioners so to do, fails to construct and keep in repair sufficient fishways or ladders on such dam or obstruction, is guilty of a misdemeanor.—[Hittell's Code, as amended to date.

Misdemeanors.—Except in cases where a different punishment is prescribed by this Code, every offense declared to be a misdemeanor is punishable by imprisonment not exceeding six months or by a fine not exceeding $500, or both. —[Penal Code, 1872, § 19.

Mocking Birds.—No person shall willfully shoot, wound, or in any manner catch any mocking bird, or take, injure, or destroy any mocking bird's eggs, in the State of California, under a fine of not less than $5 nor more than $10 and costs, for each offense.—[Act February 14, 1872.

Siskiyou County.—It is unlawful in Siskiyou county, to take, kill, or destroy any grouse, sage hen, or prairie chicken, between the 1st day of April and the 1st day of August; or any quail between the 15th day of March and the 15th day of October; or any mallard duck, wood duck, teal duck, spoonbill duck, and all other species of wild duck between the 15th day of April and the 15th day of September; or any elk, deer, antelope, or mountain sheep between the 1st day of February and the 1st day of August. Any person offending against any of the provisions of this act, or who shall buy, sell, expose for sale, or have in possession any of the game birds or animals above enumerated within the time herein specified, except such as are tamed, shall be fined $25 for each bird or animal so taken, killed, destroyed, bought, sold, or had in possession.—[Act April 2, 1866.

Nevada County.—It is unlawful to take, kill, or destroy any elk, deer, or antelope in Nevada county between the 1st day of February and the 1st day of August yearly.—[Act February 2, 1872.

Napa County.—It is unlawful to either hunt or fish in any enclosed land in that part of Napa county east of Napa River without permission from the owner theeof, under a fine of not less than $50 nor more than $500, or imprisonment from twenty days to three months, or both.—[Act March 26, 1872.

The following judicious act was passed by the legislature of California at its last session:—

§ 1. The State board of fish commissioners are hereby authorized to purchase for the purposes of propagation, import into this State, and distribute to such places within this State as may in their judgment be best suitable for the same, such game birds as they may be able to secure, including **Wild Turkeys, Prairie Chickens, Bob-White Quail, Pheasants, Grouse, Sky-larks,** and others valuable as game birds....§ 4. Any person who shall, within this State, prior to the 1st day of January, 1895, shoot, trap, kill, or otherwise destroy any bird mentioned in section one of this act is guilty of a misdemeanor, and the shooting, trapping, killing, or otherwise destroying of each of said birds shall be a separate offense.—[Chap. 210, laws 1889.

The following act, amending section 635, was also passed:—

§ 635. Any person who places or allows to pass into any of the waters of this State any lime, gas tar, cocculus indicus, sawdust, or any substance deleterious to fish, is guilty of a misdemeanor. And every person who uses any poisonous or explosive substances for the purpose of taking or destroying fish is guilty of a misdemeanor. Any person who shall catch, take, or carry away any trout or other fish from any stream, pond, or reservoir, belonging to any person or corporation, without the consent of the owner therein, which stream, pond, or reservoir, has been stocked with fish by hatching therein eggs or spawn, or by placing the same therein, is guilty of a misdemeanor.—[Chap. 65, laws 1889.

Game and Fish Laws of Colorado.

§ 1543. No person shall kill, net, ensnare or trap within this State, any **Quail, Wild Turkey, Lark**, whip-poor-will, finch, thrush, sparrow, wren, martin, swallow, snow bird, bobolink, red-winged black-bird, crow, raven, turkey buzzard, robin, or other **Insectivorous Birds**, except that **Partridge, Pheasant, Prairie Hen, Prairie Chicken**, or **Grouse** may be shot from October first to November fifteenth of each year; and if, at any time, any person shall be found in possession of any partridge, pheasant, prairie hen, prairie chicken, or grouse, at any other time than between the dates above mentioned, or any other of the fowls or birds named in this section, at any time, it shall be *prima facie* evidence that the same was killed, netted, ensnared, or trapped, by such person, in violation of the provisions of this act; provided this section shall not be construed to prohibit any person importing or dealing in quail, partridge, or prairie hen, prairie chicken, pheasant, wild turkey, or grouse imported into this State from any other State or Territory; and provided further that this shall not prohibit any **Professional Taxidermists** from killing birds or animals for preservation in cabinets or museums, and such professional taxidermists shall be exempt from the penalties of the following sections, upon making satisfactory proof that the birds or animal killed have been pre-served as aforesaid.... § 1544. Any person violating any of the provisions of this act is guilty of misdemeanor, and, upon conviction, shall be fined not less than five dollars nor more than fifty dollars, one-half of fine to be for the informer.... § 1544*a*. **Wild Fowl.**—No person shall ensnare, net, or trap, within this State, any wild duck or wild goose at any time, under same penalties as provided in preceding section.... § 1545. No person shall kill, wound, ensnare any **Bison or Buffalo**, within the State, for a period of ten (10) years, from and after the approval of this act. No person shall kill, or wound, ensnare or trap any **Mountain Sheep**, within this State, for a period of eight (8) years, from and after the approval of this act. No person shall kill or wound, ensnare or trap any **Ibex**, or **Rocky Mountain Goat**, within this State, for a period of ten (10) years, from and after the approval of this act. (Act approved March 26, 1889.) No person shall kill or wound, ensnare or trap any **Deer, Elk, Fawn** or **Antelope**, within this State, for any purpose whatever, at any time, except that those which have horns may be killed between July 1st and December 1st of the same year for food purposes, and then only when necessary for immediate use, governed in amount and quantity by the reasonable necessities of the person or persons killing such animal. Nor shall it be lawful at any time for any person to kill, ensnare or trap any deer, elk, fawn or antelope, for the sole purpose of securing the skins or horns of any such animal; and the selling or offering for sale, or the shipping, or having in possession for the purpose of transporting out of the State any of the skins or horns of such animals, shall be *prima facie* evidence that such animals were killed for such purpose; nor shall it be lawful for any person or persons or corporation to have in possession any of the game herein mentioned, except during the times above specified, for any purpose whatever. Any person or persons offending against the provisions of this section shall be deemed guilty of misdemeanor, and upon conviction thereof, as in proceeding in cases of assault and battery, before any justice of the peace, shall be fined in any sum not less than $50, nor more than $200 for the first offense, and for each subsequent offense shall be fined in any sum not less than $50, nor more than $200, and be imprisoned in the county jail not less than thirty days, nor more than ninety days. Any person arrested and brought before any justice of the peace for any violation of the provisions of this section, shall be entitled to a trial by a jury of six, unless he shall waive the same, and if the jury find him guilty the justice of the peace shall assess the fine and costs, and fix the term of imprisonment, as the case may be. One-half of the fine shall be paid to the informer, and the other half shall go to the school fund of the county. Indictments may also be found by the Grand Jury..... § 1547.—**Trespass.** It is unlawful for any person to kill, ensnare or trap, in the enclosure of any other person, any elk, deer, antelope, mountain sheep, or any game whatsoever, at any time without the consent of the owner, or to enter such enclosure with a gun for the purpose of hunting, without the consent of the owner, under a penalty not to exceed one hundred dollars, nor under twenty-five dollars for every such offense, and in default of payment, imprisonment for one day for every three dollars of the amount thereof.....§ 1548. For the more certain detection and punishment of violators of this act, the Governor of the State shall have power to appoint special game wardens, who shall hold their office during the pleasure of the Governor; it is hereby made the duty of such game wardens, so appointed, and all sheriffs and constables, or any other person of the several counties, whenever a violation of its provisions is brought to their knowledge, to file, or cause to be filed, an affidavit before a justice of the peace, charging the person or persons with the offense committed; and thereupon, a warrant shall issue for the arrest of such person or persons, and trial shall be had, as above provided. Justices of the peace are hereby empowered to appoint special constables, who, of their own knowledge, or upon the information of a reputable citizen of the county, may arrest, without warrant, any person or persons violating the provisons of this act, and take him or them before the nearest acting justice of the peace, where trial shall be had, after the proper affidavit shall have been filed, as though a warrant had issued in the first instance; and this section shall be a full protection of any such officer or person above mentioned who causes the affidavit or the arrest to be made in good faith, or upon the information of a reputable citizen of the county. Prosecutions may also be made in other courts as in other cases.

Fish.—§ 1. It is unlawful to take. or kill, or fish for any **Trout** or other fish in any of the waters of this State, within two hundred yards of any fish-way or artificial or natural obstruction, or to take or kill in any of the waters of this State any **Speckled Trout** or **Food Fish**, at any time, by the use of any poisonous or deleterious or stupefying drug, or by the use of any explosive substance, or by the erection of any weir, dam, or other artificial obstruction; or by the use of any net, seine, or device whatever, except by hook and line. It is unlawful to empty or allow the emptying of any sawdust into any of the waters of this State containing food fish, or to deposit the same within such distance that it may be carried into said waters by natural causes. But nothing herein shall be so construed as to prevent the fish commissioner from taking fish of any kind, at any time and in any manner he may choose, for the purpose of science, cultivation, and dissemination; and he may permit other persons to take fish at any time and in any manner, for the same purposes, by giving them written permits.....§ 2. It is unlawful to kill or take any trout or other fish, in any manner whatsoever, from any private lake, pond, or stream, used for the propagation of such fish, except by the consent of the proprietor of such lake, pond, or stream.....§ 3. Any person or the officers and servants of any company or corporation, maintaining or keeping up any dam or weir, or other artificial obstruction, in or upon any stream of water in this State, must erect and keep up and maintain at such dam, weir, or other artificial obstruction, a sufficient sluice or fish-way, for the free passage of fish up and down any such stream; but this section does not apply to any stream of water that contains no food fish, nor to any stream of water the whole volume of which is used for irrigating purposes.....§ 4. It is unlawful to kill, take, or have in possession any **Trout** or other **Food Fish**, taken or killed in any of the public waters of this State for any purpose except for food, and then only, when necessary for immediate use, governed in amount and quantity by the reasonable necessities of the person catching such fish. Any person violating this section shall be fined, upon conviction, not less than $50 nor more than $100.—[Session laws 1887.....§ 5. Any person or the officers or servants of any company or corporation, violating any of the provisions of this act is guilty of a misdemeanor, and, on conviction, shall be fined not less than $50 nor more than $300; provided, however, that any person convicted of using any poison or deleterious or stupefying drug or by the use of any explosive substance for the purpose of taking or killing any food fish in any of the waters of this State, shall, upon conviction thereof, be fined not less than $100 nor more than $300 for each and every offense, or be imprisoned for not more than sixty days, or both.—[As amended by laws 1881. All acts conflicting herewith have been repealed.—[Chap. 37, laws 1887, containing all amendments made thereto up to date of publication.

Game and Fish Laws of North and South Dakota.

NOTE.—George F. Goodwin, Attorney General for North Dakota, writes under date of Jan. 20, 1890, that all Territorial Laws, for the whole Territory of Dakota, in force at the time of the adoption of the Constitution, are still in force.

§ 1. It is unlawful to kill, ensnare, or trap, in any form or manner or by any device whatever, or for any purpose, any **Buffalo, Elk, Deer, Antelope,** or **Mountain Sheep**, between the 1st day of January and the 1st day of September of each and every year, under a penalty of $10 for each elk and $100 for each deer, antelope, or mountain sheep so killed or found in possession....§2. It is unlawful in this Territory, to shoot or kill any **Prairie Chicken**, or **Pinnated Grouse,** or **Sharp-Tailed Grouse**, or **Ruffled Grouse** between the 1st day of January and the 1st day of September, or any **Wild Duck, Snipe, Goose, Brant, Plover,** or **Curlew** between the 15th day of May and the 1st day of September, or any **Song Bird** at any time....§ 3. It is unlawful at any time or at any place in this Territory to shoot or kill for traffic any prairie chicken, wild duck, snipe, goose, brant, plover, or curlew, or for any person to shoot or kill during one day more than twenty-five of either kind of said named birds, or for any one person, firm, or corporation to have more than twenty-five of said named birds in possession at any one time, unless lawfully received for transportation, or at any time to catch or take, or attempt to catch or take, with any trap, snare, or net, any of the birds named in section two of this act, or in any manner willfully to take or destroy the eggs, or nests of any of the birds hereby intended to be protected from destruction, or to buy or sell any of said birds or their eggs.....§ 4. It is unlawful for any person, firm, or corporation to **have in possession** any of the birds named in section two during the time the killing of such birds is therein prohibited....§ 5. It is unlawful for any person, company, or corporation at any time to **Ship, Take** or **Carry** out of this Territory any of the birds named in section two of this act, but it is lawful for any person to ship to any person within this Territory, any game birds named in section two not to exceed one dozen in number in any one day during the period when by this act the killing of such birds is not prohibited; *Provided,* He shall first make an affidavit, that said birds have not been unlawfully killed, bought, sold, or had in possession, are not being shipped for sale or profit; giving the name and postoffice address of the person to whom shipped, and the number of birds to be so shipped. A copy of such affidavit endorsed "A true copy of the original," by the person administering the oath to be furnished by him to the affiant who shall deliver the same to the railroad agent or common carrier receiving such birds for transportation, and the same shall operate as a release to such carrier or agent from any liability in the shipment or carrying such birds. The original affidavit to be retained by the officer taking the same, and may be used as evidence in any prosecution for violation of this act. Any person swearing falsely to any material fact of said affidavit is guilty of perjury, and to be punished accordingly....§ 6. If any person shall shoot, kill, catch, or take, trap, ensnare, buy, sell, ship, or have in possession, or ship, take, or carry out of the Territory, contrary to the provisions of this act, any of the birds herein named, or shall willfully destroy any eggs or nests of any of such birds, such person shall be fined $10 for each bird or nest, or the eggs therein, so shot, killed, trapped, caught, or taken, ensnared, bought, sold, shipped, had in possession, destroyed, or shipped, taken, or carried out of the Territory, and to stand committed for thirty days, unless such fine be sooner paid....§ 7. If any railway, express company, or any other common carrier, or any of their agents or servants knowingly receives any of the aforementioned birds for transportation or other purpose, during the period hereinbefore limited and prohibited, or at any other time except in manner provided in section five of this act, they shall be fined not less than $100 nor more than $300, or imprisoned thirty days, or both....§ 8. If any person shall kill, or shoot any wild duck, goose, or brant, with any **Swivel Gun,** or any kind of gun, except such as is commonly shot from the shoulder, or shall use medicated or poisoned food to capture or kill any of the birds named in this act, is liable to a fine of $25 for each offense, and in default of payment, to stand committed for thirty days, unless the same be sooner paid.—[Chap. 58, laws 1887.

Large Game.—Unlawful to Transport.—It is unlawful to ship, for any purpose whatsoever, from the Territory of Dakota, the carcase of any buffalo, elk, deer, antelope, or mountain sheep, under a penalty of $50 for each carcase shipped.

Quail.—It is unlawful to kill, trap, or destroy, by any means whatever, any quail in the Territory of Dakota for two years from March 5, 1887, under a penalty of $10 for each quail so killed, trapped, or destroyed.—Chapter 59, laws 1887.

Beaver.—It is unlawful to kill, entrap, ensnare, capture, or destroy any beaver in the Territory of Dakota for five years from the 11th day of March, 1887, under a penalty not to exceed $100, or imprisonment not to exceed thirty days or both.—[Chap. 60, laws 1887.

Fish.—It is unlawful to take, catch, kill, or destroy any fish whatever, except by angling with hook and line, in any of the lakes or streams, or inlets or outlets of said streams, or any of the waters of Dakota Territory, except the Missouri and Red Rivers. It is unlawful to take, catch, kill, or destroy, by any device whatsoever, any **Pike Pickerel, Perch, Bass, or Muscalonge**—except for the purposes of breeding and propagating—in any of the waters of Dakota Territory, except in Missouri and Red Rivers, between the 1st day of February and the 1st day of May in any year, or to expose the same for sale during this period. Any violation of the foregoing provisions is punishable by a fine of not less than $5 nor more than $25 for the first offense, and not less than $10 nor more than $100, or imprisonment not exceeding thirty days, or both, for each subsequent offense. All inconsistent acts are repealed.—[Chap. 60, laws 1883.

Public Stocked Waters.—Any person taking from the public waters of Dakota, except for breeding purposes, any fish or spawn which may have been placed therein for breeding purposes, or for the purpose of stocking such waters with food fishes, until public notice shall have been given by the Territorial commissioner of fish and fisheries that the same are open to the public for food purposes, is liable to a penalty not exceeding $100.—[Chap. 60, laws 1883.

Game and Fish Laws of Kansas.

§ 1. It is unlawful, at any time, excepting as hereinafter provided, to catch, kill, trap, net, or ensnare, or pursue with such intent, any **Wild Bird**, except the wild goose, duck, hawk, harrier, crow, bluejay, snipe, curlew, plover, bittern, heron, crane, and woodpecker.....§ 2. *It is Lawful to Shoot* or take possession of any **Pinnated Grouse** or **Prairie Chicken** between the 1st day of September and the 1st day of January of each and every year. It is, however, unlawful to net, catch, trap, or ensnare said birds at any time. But it is provided that *It is Lawful for any Person to Shoot Quail on his own premises* between the 1st day of November and the 1st day of January.....§ 3. It is unlawful at any time, to hunt or pursue any wild bird or game upon the occupied or improved premises of another, or upon any traveled or public road that adjoins such occupied or improved premises, without having obtained permission or consent of the owner or occupant thereof.....§ 4. It is unlawful for any person, company, or corporation to *Buy, Sell, or Barter within the State of Kansas, any Birds* not excepted in section one, or the birds enumerated in section two when the shooting thereof is prohibited. And the having in possession by any person, company, or corporation of any such birds, when the shooting, catching, or killing thereof is prohibited, is *prima facie* evidence of the violation of this act. It is provided, however, that nothing herein shall be so construed as to prevent any person from purchasing from another person who has legally killed the same, any of the birds mentioned in said chapter 115, laws of 1883, for use as food in his own family, or from selling the same by any person having lawfully killed the same to any person for use in his own family.—[Chap. 110, laws 1886.... § 5. Any person convicted of violating any of the foregoing provisions is liable to a penalty of not less than $5 nor more than $25 for each offense, to stand committed till paid.....§ 7. It is not necessary to prove on the trial or to state in the

complaint the true name of the bird caught or killed in violation of this act....
§ 8. The provisions of this act do not apply to any person who shall kill or
catch any wild bird for the sole purpose of preserving the same as specimens
for scientific purposes.....§ 9. All acts or parts of acts inconsistent herewith
are repealed.—[Chap. 115, laws 1883, as amended 1886.

It is unlawful to catch, or attempt to catch, or to kill, any fish in any of the
inland waters of the State of Kansas by *Poisoning the Water* with lime, or any
deleterious substance whatever, or by making any obstruction to the natural
transit of fish for the purpose of catching the same. It is unlawful to catch, or
attempt to catch, or to kill, any **Black Bass, Croppies, Perch,** or **Wall-Eyed Pike** by
means of any drag-net, gill-net, drift-net, trammel-net, seine, fish-pot, set-net,
wire pond, or any device whatever, *Except by Rod, Line, and Hook.* It is unlawful
to catch any other kind of fish not mentioned herein at any time, except during
May and June of each year. Section two of chapter 108, laws of 1886, is repealed.—[Laws 1889.

Game and Fish Laws of Montana.

§ 1. Any person who shall willfully shoot, or otherwise kill, or cause to be
killed, any **Buffalo, Elk, Moose,** White-Tailed or Black-Tailed Deer, **Mountain Sheep,
Rocky Mountain Goat,** or **Antelope,** between the 1st day of December and the 15th
day of August of the ensuing year, shall be fined, on conviction, not less than
$20 nor more than $50 for each offense committed....§ 2. Any person who shall
willfully shoot, or otherwise kill or cause to be killed at any time, any of the
animals mentioned in section one of this act, for the purpose of securing the
Head or Hide only, or for *Speculative Purposes* or *Market,* or *For Sale,* shall be
fined, upon conviction, not less than $50 nor more than $200, or imprisonment not
less than one month nor more than three months, or both....§ 3. No person shall
kill or cause to be killed, any **Beaver, Otter,** or **Fisher** between the 1st day of April
and the 1st day of October, nor at any time catch any beaver in any inclosure
(but nothing contained in this section shall prevent any person from catching
or killing beaver on their own lands) ; nor (§ 4) any of the varieties of **Wild
Geese** or **Ducks** which at any season of the year are found in this Territory between the 15th day of May and the 10th day of August.....§ 5. Any person who
shall willfully shoot, or cause to be killed, any Grouse, Prairie Chicken, **Pheasant,
Fool Hen, Sage Hen, Partridge,** or **Quail** between the 15th day of November and the
15th day of August next ensuing, shall be fined, on conviction, not less than $25
nor more than $50, and the killing of any of said birds for *Speculative Purposes,*
or *For Market,* or *For Sale,* is at all times prohibited ; and any person who shall
kill any of the kinds of birds mentioned in this section for speculative purposes or for sale, shall, on conviction, be fined not less than $25 nor more than
$50 for each offense.....§ 6. Any person who shall willfully shoot, kill, or cause
to be killed, any wild geese or wild ducks between the 1st day of May and the
15th day of August of each year, shall, upon conviction, be fined not less than
$10 nor more than $25 for each offense.....§ 7. Any person who shall willfully
shoot, or otherwise kill, or in any manner whatever cause to be killed, any robin,
meadowlark, flecker, or yellowhammer, oriole, mocking bird, goldfinch, snow-
bird, cedar-bird, or any of the small birds known as **Singing Birds** shall be fined, on
conviction, not less than $5 nor more than $10 for each offense.—[Laws of 1883.
....§ 7. Possession of the dead bodies, or any part thereof, of any of the animals or birds mentioned in this act is *prima facie* evidence that the possessor
killed the same.....§ 8. Fishing tackle, consisting of a rod or pole, line and
hook, or spear is the only lawful way in which fish can be taken in any of the
streams of this Territory; but a seine may be used, however, in the Missouri or
Jefferson Rivers, and in the Beaver Head up to the Beaver Head Rock, and in
North Boulder Creek for ten miles from its mouth.....§ 9. Any violation of
this section is punishable by a fine of not less than $50 nor more than $250.
The complainant is entitled to one-half of all fines when collected.—[Laws 1887.

Quail.—It is unlawful to kill by any means any quail in this Territory which
have been turned loose for the purpose of propagation and domestication, or
to kill the increase of quail for six years from March 12, 1885, under a penalty
of $25.—[Laws 1885.

Transportation of Game.—It is unlawful to ship, transport, or receive for transportation, carry or cause to be carried in any manner whatsoever, from the Territory of Montana to any other Territory or State, the skin of any moose, deer, elk, bison or buffalo, antelope, or mountain sheep, and any person, company, corporation, agent, or employe of any stage, railway, or express company violating the provisions of this act, shall, on conviction, be fined not less than $50 nor more than $300, or imprisoned for not less than thirty days nor more than six months; but nothing herein shall prevent the shipment of any specimens that are stuffed or mounted as curiosities.—[Act March 12, 1885.

The following are amendments recently made to the laws of Montana.—

§ 1. Any person who shall willfully shoot or otherwise kill for ten years from and after the passage of this act, any **Bison, Buffalo, or Quail**, or who shall willfully shoot or otherwise kill for six years, from and after the passage of this act, any **Moose, Elk, Beaver**, within this Territory, shall be deemed guilty of a misdemeanor, and be fined not less than $200 nor more than $500, or be imprisoned not less than two months nor more than six months, or both for each offense, and the possession of the skin or meat of any of the above mentioned animals killed during said period shall be presumptive evidence that the person having either in possession, killed the same in violation of this section. The provisions of this section shall not be deemed or held to apply to persons who raise buffalo.

....§ 2. Any person who shall willfully shoot, or otherwise kill or cause to be killed, any **White-Tailed Deer, Black-Tailed Deer, Mule Deer, Mountain Sheep, Rocky Mountain Goat**, or **Antelope**, between the 1st day of January and the 15th day of September of the same year, shall be deemed guilty of a misdemeanor, and, upon conviction thereof, be fined in any sum not less than $20 nor more than $50 for each offense committed.

Fish.—§ 3. That a fishing tackle consisting of a rod or pole, line, hook, or spear shall be the only lawful way that fish can be taken in any of the rivers, streams, lakes and ponds of this Territory. Said hook shall not be baited with any poisonous drug or substance, and it is unlawful for any person to make any dams or use any fish traps, grab-hooks, or similar means for catching fish, or to use any drugs or poison or giant powder or other explosive compound, intending to catch, kill, or destroy fish of any species; but nothing herein contained shall prevent the use of any seine or other catch net used to catch fish in any river or stream below two hundred miles from the head of any such river or stream; provided, that such seine or catch net shall have a mesh not less than one inch square. And any person, company, or corporation, offending against this section shall be deemed guilty of a misdemeanor, and, upon conviction thereof, shall be fined not exceeding $250, or be imprisoned for not more than six months, and costs.....§ 4. All laws and parts of laws in conflict with this act be and the same are hereby repealed.—[Act of 1889.

Game and Fish Laws of Nebraska.

§ 83. INSECTIVOROUS OR SONG BIRDS.—It is unlawful, in the State of Nebraska, to knowingly or intentionally kill, injure, or harm, except upon the land owned by such persons, any robin, thrush, lark, blue-birds, king-bird, sparrow, wren, jay, swallow, turtle-dove, oriole, woodpecker, yellowhammer, cuckoo, yellow-bird, bobolink, or other bird or birds of like nature, that promote agriculture or horticulture by feeding on noxious worms and insects and that are attractive in appearance or cheerful in song, under a penalty of not less than $3 nor more than $10 for each bird injured or harmed.....§ 84. It is unlawful, between the 15th day of April and the 15th day of February following, to catch, trap, kill, or to pursue with such intent, on the premises of another, any **Muskrat, Mink** or **Otter**, or at any time to enter upon the premises of another without his consent, with a view of trapping, hunting, killing, or pursuing, with the intent of killing any such animals, or to enter upon the premises of another without his consent, and destroy, tear down, or in any manner injure the muskrat heaps or houses on such premises, under a penalty not exceeding $20 for each offense; provided that this section is not to be so construed as to prevent the catching, and killing of any animal herein specified where there is danger of their doing damage to property, either public or private.....§ 85.

Wild Fowl, Punt Guns, etc.—It is unlawful at any time, by the aid or use of any swivel, punt gun, big gun (so called), or any other gun than the common shoulder gun or by the aid or use of any punt-boat or sneak-boat, used for carrying such gun, to catch, kill, wound, or destroy upon any of the waters bays, rivers, marshes, mud-flats, or any cover to which wild fowl resort within the State of Nebraska, or any wild goose, wood duck, teal, canvas back, bluebill, or other wild duck, or to destroy or disturb the eggs of any of the birds above named, under a penalty of not less than $2 nor more than $20 for each offense, or imprisonment not exceeding twenty days, or both.....§ 86. It is unlawful to kill, ensnare or trap any **Buffalo, Elk, Mountain Sheep, Deer** or **Antelope** (except for the purpose of domestication), between the 1st day of January and the 1st day of October in any year; or to kill, ensnare, or trap any **Wild Grouse** between the 1st day of January and the 1st day of September in each year; or any **Quail** or **Wild Turkey** between the 1st day of January and the 1st day of October in each year; or **Ensnare, Trap,** or **Net** the same at any time of the year; or to **Buy, Sell, Ship, Transport, Carry,** or **Have in Possession**, any such animal or bird between the dates within which the killing, ensnaring, trapping, or netting of such animals or birds is prohibited by law. It is unlawful for any person, agent or employee of any association, corporation, railroad or express company to receive, carry, transport or ship any such animal or bird at any time of the year. **Trespass.**—It is unlawful to go upon the premises of any person or corporation, for the purpose of hunting, trapping, netting, ensnaring, or killing any animal or bird at any season of the year, unless by consent of the owner or owners of said premises. Any person, agent, or employee, as aforesaid, who shall violate any provision of this section, is guilty of a misdemeanor, and upon conviction shall be fined $15 for each buffalo, elk, mountain sheep, deer, antelope, or wild turkey, and $5 for each grouse or quail, so as aforesaid killed, trapped, ensnared, netted, bought, sold, shipped, transported or held in possession in violation of the provisions of this section. Having in possession any of the named animals or birds between said dates, is presumptive evidence that the same were killed, ensnared, netted or trapped in violation of this section. Any person who shall go upon the land of another, in violation of this section, shall, upon conviction thereof, be fined for such offense any sum not less than $5 nor more than $50, and shall be liable to the owner or owners of the premises for an action for trespass.

Chasing Deer with Dogs.—If any person within the counties of *Burt, Washington, Douglass, Sarpy, Cass, Jaunders,* and *Dodge* shall chase or pursue any deer with any hound or dog, such person shall, upon conviction, be fined $20, or imprisoned not less than ten nor more than twenty days.—[Chap. —, Gen. Stat., 1873.

§ 24. **Wolves, Wild Cats, Mountain Lions, and Coyotes**—*State Bounty.*—A bounty of $1 is paid for every wolf, wild cat, or coyote killed within the boundaries of the State of Nebraska. The scalps of said animals with the two ears and face down to the nose, must be presented to the county clerk of the county wherein said animals were killed, with satisfactory proof, on oath, that the same were killed within the boundaries of the State of Nebraska....§ 27. Any person driving, enticing, bringing, or taking any of said animals from outside the boundaries of the State, or from any one unorganized territory in this State into any organized county, for the purpose of procuring bounties thereon, shall be fined not less than $25 nor more than $100 for each offense....§ 29. *County Bounty.*—A bounty of $3 for every wolf or mountain lion, and a bounty of $1 for every wild cat or coyote is paid by such counties as may at any election, so determine by a majority of voters voting....§ 32. The provisions respecting scalps are similar to section 24....§ 32. Any person driving, baiting, enticing, bringing or taking any of said animals from outside the ,boundaries of such counties as are provided for in this act, for the purpose of obtaining bounties on such animals, shall be fined in any sum not less than $25 nor more than $50 for each and every offense committed.—[Chap. 4, Animals] Gen. Stats., 1885.

§ 87. **Private Ponds.**—It is unlawful to catch, interfere with, injure, or in any manner to destroy or maliciously disturb, to the damage of the private property of another, the fish in, or work connected with any private fish pond, not exceeding ten acres, in this State, under a penalty of not less than $10 nor more than $200. It is lawful to take up, remove, or clear away, any fish-net, seine, or fish pound placed in the waters of any lake or pond contrary to the provisions of this act....§ 8:a. **Fish, Nets, Etc.**—It is unlawful to catch, kill, injure, or destroy any fish in any river, creek, brook, stream, lake, pond, bayou, or other body of water in this State, with a seine, trammel net, gill net, pound net, basket, weir, or in any other manner whatever, except by hook and line, spear, and fork. It is unlawful to set, place, deposit, or drag a seine, or net of any description, or basket or weir, in any of the above-named waters in this State, and every seine, net, basket, or weir found in any waters of this State, may be taken up by any one; but nothing herein shall be so construed as to prohibit the owners of private ponds or streams taking fish therein at any time or in any manner. Every person violating any provision of this section, shall, upon conviction thereof, be fined not less than $5 for each offense, or imprisoned not less than ten days, or both....§ 87b. It is unlawful to injure, disturb, or destroy any hatching-box, hatching-house or pond, used for hatching or propagating fish, or to injure, destroy, or disturb any spawn or fry, or fish in any hatching-box, hatching-house, pond, or stream; but the fish commissioners of this State may take or cause to be taken any of the fish named in this section for the purpose of propagation or stocking the waters of the State. Every person violating any provision of this section, shall be fined not more than $10 for each fish taken, or held in possession, or other offense under this section, or imprisonment not more than ten days, or both....§ 87c. It is unlawful to catch, injure, kill, or destroy any **California Salmon, Land-locked Salmon, Trout, Shad, White-Fish, or Carp,** which have been planted or placed in any of the waters of this State by the fish commissioners, or by private persons, under a penalty of not less than $10 for each fish so taken, injured, killed, destroyed, or had in possession, or imprisonment not less than ten days, or both. The having in possession any fish named in this section is presumptive evidence that the same were taken in violation of law....§ 88. All acts conflicting herewith are repealed.—[Chap. 9, Gen. Stat., 1885.

Game and Fish Laws of Nevada.

Insectivorous Birds ...§ 1. It is unlawful, at any time to kill or injure any sparrow, blue-bird, bluejay, martin, thrush, mocking-bird, swallow, redbreast, cat-bird, wren, or humming-bird, or to disturb the nest or eggs of said birds ....§ 2. It is unlawful between the 1st day of April and the 1st day of September following, to catch, kill, or destroy any **Partridge, Pheasant, Woodcock, Quail,** or any **Wild Goose, Wild Duck, Teal, Mallard,** or other ducks, **Sandhill Crane, Brant, Swan, Plover, Curlew, Snipe, Grouse, Robin, Meadow Lark, Yellowhammer,** or **Buttern;** and after the 1st day of April and before the 1st day of September of each year (except in the counties of Humbolt, Elko, Eureka, and Lander, as hereinafter provided), any **Sage Cock, Hen, or Chicken** ....§ 3. It is unlawful in this State, at any time to trap or net quail, or to destroy, injure, or disturb the nest or eggs of any of the birds protected by this act....§ 4. It is unlawful to catch, kill, or destroy, within the limits of Esmeralda, Douglas, Ormsby, Lyon, Churchill, Storey, and Washoe counties any **Sharp-tailed Grouse** (so called prairie chicken), before the 1st day of September, or within the limits of Humboldt, Elko, Eureka and Lander counties after the 15th day of March and before the 1st day of September, or in said last named counties any **Sage-Cock, Hen, or Chicken** after the 15th day of March and before the 10th day of August in each year....§ 5. It is unlawful at any time after the 1st day of January and before the 1st day of September in each year to catch, kill, or destroy any **Deer, Antelope, Elk, Mountain Sheep, or Goat,** or to have in possession, expose for sale, or purchase any of the animals mentioned in this section during the season when the killing, injuring, or pursuing is herein prohibited....§ 6. It is unlawful within this State to have in possession, expose for sale, or purchase, either from Indians or any other person, any of the birds, wild game, or animals mentioned in this act, during the season wherein the killing, injuring, or pursuing is herein prohibited; but nothing in this act shall be so construed as to prohibit the taking of any bird, fowl, fish, or animal at any time for scientific purposes....§ 7. Every person violating any of the provisions of this act is liable, on conviction, to a fine of not less than $25 nor more than $200 or imprisonment not exceeding six months, or both .. § 8. All acts in conflict herewith are repealed.—[Chap. 219, laws 1887.

Beaver and Otter.—It is unlawful in the State of Nevada to trap or kill any beaver or otter before the 1st day of April, 1897, under a penalty of not less than $25 nor more than $200, or imprisonment not exceeding two months, or both.—[Chap. 38, laws 1887.

Fish.—It is unlawful between the 1st day of January and the 1st day of September of each year to catch or kill any **River, Lake, Brook, or Salmon Trout** in any of the waters within this State, in any manner, except by hook and line. It is unlawful *at any time* to catch or kill such fish by any poisonous, deleterious or stupefying drug, explosive material, or other substance. Any person violating any of the foregoing provisions is liable, on conviction, to a fine of not less than $30 nor exceeding $300 or imprisonment for not less than twenty days nor more than six months, or both.—[Act March 2, 1871.

Humboldt River.—It is unlawful to catch or kill *in any manner whatever*, or to induce, cause, or employ any person to do so, any of the fish within the **Humboldt River**, or any of the tributaries thereto, from the 1st day of January to the 1st day of May following. It is unlawful for any person from the 1st day of July to the 1st day of December following of each year to sell, expose for sale, buy, procure, or accept for any consideration from any person whatever, any of the fish caught or killed in the **Humboldt River** or any of the tributaries thereof. Any violation of the provisions of this act is punishable by a fine of not over $50 or imprisonment not exceeding three months, or both.—[Laws 1887.

Game and Fish Laws of Oregon.

§ 1. Every person who shall within the State of Oregon, hunt, pursue, take, kill or destroy, any **Male Deer,** or **Buck,** between the 1st day of November in each year, and the 1st day of July of the following year, or any **Female Deer,** or **Doe,** for a period of four years from the passage of this act, or any **Spotted Fawn,** or who shall kill any male or female deer or buck at any time, unless the carcass of such animal is used or preserved by the person slaying it, or is sold for food, is guilty of a misdemeanor.... § 2. Every person who buys, sells, or has in possession, any of the deer enumerated in the preceding section, within the time the taking or killing thereof is prohibited, except such as are tamed or kept for show or curiosity, is guilty of a misdemeanor....§ 3. Every person who shall between the 1st day of November and the 1st day of August of the ensuing year, hunt, pursue, take, kill, or destroy any **Elk, Moose,** or **Mountain Sheep,** or who takes, kills, injures, or destroys, or pursues with such intent, any elk, moose, mountain sheep, or deer at any time, for the sole purpose of obtaining the skin, hide or hams of any such animal, is guilty of a misdemeanor. Every person who shall sell, or offer for sale, barter or exchange, and every person or corporation who shall buy, or offer to buy, or transport or carry for the purpose of barter or sale or exchange, the skin or hide of any moose, elk, deer, or mountain sheep, shall be guilty of a misdemeanor; and every person who shall sell or offer for sale, or buy or offer to buy, or have in his possession or custody, or under his control, any elk, deer, moose, or mountain sheep, at any time when it is unlawful to take or kill the same, shall be guilty of a misdemeanor, and upon the prosecution of any person or persons for a violation of any of the provisions of this act, the possession by the accused of any of the aforesaid animals at any time when it is unlawful to take or kill the same, and the possession by the accused of any such hide or skin at any time, shall be *prima facie* evidence of the guilt of the accused.....§ 4. Every person who shall take, kill, injure or destroy, or have in possession, sell or offer for sale, any **Wild Swan, Mallard Duck, Wood Duck, Widgeon, Teal, Spoonbill, Gray, Black,** or **Sprigtail Duck,** between the 1st of April and the 1st of September (provided that any person may at any time kill ducks to protect his growing crops) or (§ 5) any **Prairie Chicken** or **Sage Hen,** for any purpose, between the 1st day of April and the 15th day of June: or (§ 6) any **Grouse, Pheasant, Quail,** or **Partridge,** between the 1st day of January and the 15th day of July; or (§ 7) who shall catch, kill, or have in possession, sell or offer for sale, any **Mountain** or **Brook Trout**, during November, December, January, February, or March of any year; or who shall at any time take, or attempt to take, or catch, with any device other than hook and line, any mountain or brook trout; or (§ 8) who shall at any time trap, net, or ensnare, or attempt to trap, net, or ensnare, any **Quail** or **Bob White, Prairie Chicken, Grouse,** or **Pheasant,** or have in possession any live quail or bob white, prairie chicken, grouse, or pheasant; or (§ 9) who shall at any time destroy or remove from the nest of any mallard duck, widgeon, wood duck, teal, spoonbill, gray, black, or sprigtail duck, prairie chicken, or sage hen, grouse, pheasant, quail, partridge, or other wild fowls, any egg or eggs of such fowls or birds, or have in possession, sell or offer for sale any such egg or eggs, or willfully destroy the nest of such fowl or birds; or (§ 10) who shall have in possession any male deer or buck, or any female deer or doe, or spotted fawn, elk, moose, or mountain sheep, swan, mallard duck, wood duck, widgeon, teal, spoonbill, gray, black, or sprigtail duck, prairie chicken, or sage hen, grouse, pheasant, quail, bob white, or partridge, mountain or brook trout, at any time when it is unlawful to take or kill the same, as provided in this act is guilty of a misdemeanor, and proof of the possession of any of the aforesaid animals, fowls, birds, or fish at a time when it is unlawful to take or kill the same, in the county where the same is found, is *prima facie* evidence in any prosecution for a violation of any of the provisions of this act, that the person or persons in whose possession the same is found, took, killed, or destroyed the same in the county wherein the same is found, during the period when it was unlawful to take, kill, or destroy the same.... § 12. Every person convicted of a violation of any of the provisions of this act shall be punished by a fine of not less than $10 and not more than $300, or imprisonment in the county jail of the county where the offense was committed, for not less than five days nor more than three months, or both such fine and imprisonment. All money collected for fines for violation of the provisions of this act shall be paid to the school fund of the county wherein such conviction is had.—[Act of 1886, as found in Hill's Code, and as amended by act of 1889.

Game and Fish Laws of Utah Territory.

Elk, Mountain Sheep, and Antelope.—Any person who willfully takes, kills, or destroys any elk, mountain sheep, or antelope is guilty of a misdemeanor.— [Chap. 3, laws 1886.

§ 1. Every person who between the 15th day of March and the 15th day of September in each year willfully takes, kills, or destroys, or offers for sale any kind of **Wild Geese** or **Wild Ducks**, or who shall at any time rob the nest of the above mentioned birds, or who shall kill any wild geese or ducks between one hour after sunset and one hour before sunrise shall be guilty of a violation of this section.....§ 2. Any person who shall, within four years, kill any bird generally known and designated as **Imported Quail**, or who shall have the dead bodies of any such birds, killed within this Territory, in possession within the confines of the Territory of Utah, shall be guilty of a violation of this section. ....§ 3. Any person violating any of the provisions of either section one or section two shall be fined not less than $10 nor more than $50.....§ 4. Every person who between the 15th day of November of each year and the 15th day of August following, takes, kills, or destroys any **Deer**, or who shall, at any time, kill any of the above animals for their skins, is guilty of a misdemeanor.....§ 5. Every person who puts into the waters of this Territory any **Poisonous Substance, Giant Powder,** or **Explosives**, upon conviction thereof, shall be fined in any sum not less than $100, or imprisonment not less than one hundred days, or may be punished by both fine and imprisonment.....§ 6. It is a misdemeanor to take out of this Territory any game taken or killed within its boundaries—Sections one and two of the laws of 1884 have been repealed.—[Laws 1888.

§ 3. Every person who buys, sells, or has in possession any of the game enumerated in the two preceding sections, taken or killed within the time during which the taking or killing thereof is forbidden (except those kept for show or curiosity), and every person who buys, sells, or offers for sale the skin of any

animal, the killing of which is herein prohibited, is guilty of a misdemeanor.
....§ 4. Every person who, at any time, takes or kills any **Fish**, except with hook and line, or with seine as hereinafter provided, or who shall catch or kill any **Trout** in any way between the 15th day of March and the 15th day of June of each year, or who willfully kills or destroys any **Trout** less than six inches long or has in possession trout taken unlawfully, is guilty of a misdemeanor; provided, that seines not more than two hundred yards long and twelve feet wide, with meshes not less than one and one-half inches square for fifty yards in the center, and meshes not less than two inches square in the wings or ends thereof may be used in Green River and Bear and Utah lakes, only between the 1st day of October of each year and the 1st day of June following; but nothing in this act shall be so construed as to prevent any person from taking fish from the public waters of this Territory for the purpose of stocking private fish ponds, or to prohibit any person from managing and controlling his private ponds or taking fish therefrom.....§ 5. Every person who, at any time, catches or kills any fish with set line or lines is guilty of a misdemeanor.....§ 6. Every person who puts into the waters of this Territory any *Poisonous* or *Explosive Substance*, or anything that is injurious to fish, or that renders the water unfit for household purposes, is guilty of a misdemeanor.....§ 7. Ever person who at any time shall take any fish from any *Private Pond* or *Stream* without the consent of the owner, is guilty of a misdemeanor.....§ 8. Every person, corporation, or association, who constructs or continues to keep any dam across any of the streams of this Territory, in which fish migrate, in such a manner as to hinder or obstruct the migration of fish to or from their spawning ground, without providing a fishway and keeping it in repair as provided in the following section, is guilty of a misdemeanor.....§ 9. The *Fishways* for the passage of fish, mentioned in the preceding section, must be made in the form of a box, open at each end, not less than four feet wide and three feet high, and of a plank not less than two inches thick, and it must be fastened in the water at the top of the dam, and the lower end must extend to and be fastened in the pool below the dam at an angle not exceeding thirty-five degrees. Inside the box, fastened at the bottom and one end to the side of the box, there must be pieces of plank four feet apart, placed transversely, so as to cause a ripple, not less than ten inches high. These pieces of plank must be thirty inches long, and so fastened as to be at right angles with the side of the box, alternately fastened one at one side, the other at the other side of the box. Whenever the stream is small the county court of the county in which the dam is to be constructed, may permit the box to be of less dimensions.....§ 11. This act applies to Indians who kill deer for their skins.—[Chap. 6, laws of 1884 and 1886.

Game and Fish Laws of Washington.

1. Every person who shall pursue, hunt, take, kill or destroy any **Deer** or **Fawn** between the 15th day of January and the 15th day of August, or who takes, kills or destroys any deer at any time, unless the carcass of such animal is used or preserved by the person slaying it, or is sold for food, or who shall hunt or pursue any deer with dogs in the counties of San Juan, Whatcom, Island, Mason, Cowlitz, Kitsap and Kittitas, or (2) who shall buy, sell or have in possession, any deer or fawn, within the time the taking or killing thereof is herein prohibited, except such as are tamed or kept for show or curiosity; or (3) who shall hunt, pursue, take, kill or destroy any **Elk, Moose,** or **Mountain Sheep** between the 1st day of January and the 15th day of August, or who shall at any time take, kill, injure, destroy or pursue any of said animals for the sole purpose of obtaining their skins, hams, cutlets; or (4) who shall take, kill, injure or destroy or have in possession, sell or offer for sale any **Wild Swan, Mallard Duck, Wood Duck,** Widgeon, Teal, Butterball, Spoonbill, Grayblack, Sprigtail or Canvas **Back Duck** between the 1st day of April and the 15th day of August; or (5) who shall for any purpose take, kill, injure or destroy or have in possession, sell or offer for sale any **Prairie Chicken, Sage Hen, Grouse, Pheasant, Partridge** or **Quail** between the 1st day of February and the 1st day of September; or (6) who shall catch, kill, have in possession, sell or offer for sale any **Mountain** or **Brook Trout** during the months of November, December, January, February and March of any year or

who shall take or attempt to take or catch with any seine, net, weir or other than hook or line any Mountain Trout or Bull Trout or Salmon Trout at any time; or (7) who shall at any time destroy or remove from the nest of any **Mallard Duck, Widgeon, Wood Duck, Teal, Butterball, Spoonbill, Grayblack, Sprigtail or Canvas Back Duck, Prairie Chicken, Sage Hen, Grouse, Pheasant, Quail or Partridge**, any egg or eggs, or willfully destroy the nest of any such fowls or birds; or (8) who shall have any male deer or buck, or any female deer or doe, or spotted fawn, elk, moose, or mountain sheep, swan, mallard duck, wood duck, widgeon, teal, butterball, spoonbill, grayblack, sprigtail or canvas back duck, prairie chicken, sage hen, grouse, pheasant, quail or bob white, partridge, mountain or brook trout at any time when it is unlawful to take or kill the same, as provided in this act; or(9) who shall take, kill, shoot at, maim or destroy any mallard duck, wood duck, widgeon, butter ball, spoonbill, grayblack, sprigtail, or canvas back duck, at any time between the hours of 8 P. M. and 5 A. M.; or (10) who shall use any sink-box on any lake or river, or other waters, for the purpose of shooting ducks or geese, or other water fowls therefrom, or who shall use any batteries, swivel or pivot gun on boats, canvas, rafts or other device at any time, for the purpose of killing any water fowl within the limits of this State, shall be guilty of misdemeanor and punishable as provided herein. Any person or persons convicted of the violation of any of the provisions of this act shall be punished by a fine of not less than $10 and not more than $300, or imprisonment in the county jail of the county where the offense was committed, for not less than five days, nor more than three months, or both such imprisonment and fine. One-half of all money collected for fines for violation of the provisions of this act shall be paid to informers, and one-half to the prosecuting attorney in the district in which the case is prosecuted. All acts or parts of acts in conflict herewith are repealed. —[Approved Nov. 27, 1883.

Salmon.—§ 1172. It is unlawful to use any seine or other apparatus during March, April, and May within the following limits: commencing at the head of Port Madison Bay in section 4, township 24 north, range 2 east, following the northern shore of said bay to Agate Passage, thence following the shore line of Bainbringe Island to Fletcher's Bay, in section 19, township 25 north, range 2 east; also the shore line of Dogfish Bay, under a penalty not exceeding $100. .. § 1173. All dams or other obstructions must be provided with suitable fishways, under a penalty of not more than $500, or imprisonment not over one year, or both .. § 1177. Traps or weirs placed in any estuary or tributary of Puget Sound must not extend across more than three-quarters of the width of the stream where placed, under a penalty of $200 to $500. ..§ 1178. Any person exploding cartridges of giant or hercules powder, dynamite, nitro-glycerine, or other explosive matter, for the purpose of catching, killing, or destroying fish within the waters named in the foregoing section, or any tributaries thereof, is guilty of a misdemeanor, and liable to a fine of not less than $100 nor more than $300....§ 1179. It is unlawful to take, or fish for salmon in the Columbia River or its tributaries by any means whatever in any year hereafter, during March and August, or at the weekly close time in April, May, June, and July; that is to say, between the hours of 6 o'clock in the afternoon of each Saturday until 6 o'clock of the afternoon of Sunday following; and any person catching salmon in violation of the provisions of this section, or purchasing salmon so unlawfully caught, is liable to a fine of not less than $500 nor more than $1000, or imprisonment not exceeding one year, or both.. § 1180. It is unlawful to fish for salmon in the Columbia River or its tributaries, during April, May, June, and July, with gill-nets, the meshes of which are less than four and one-eighth inches square, nor with seines whose meshes are less than three inches square, nor with weir or fish-traps whose slats are less than two and one-half inches apart. Nothing herein contained prevents fishing in said river and its tributaries with dip-nets during the fishing season, as defined by section 1179 ... § 1181. Every trap or weir must have an opening at least one foot wide, extending upward in that part thereof where the fish are usually taken, from the bottom to the top of the weir or trap, five feet, and the netting slats, or other materials used to close such aperture while fishing, must be taken out, carried upon the shore, and there remain during March and August and the weekly close time in April, May, June, and July as perscribed in section 1180, that the fish may have free and unobstructed passage through such weir, trap, or other structure, and no contrivance must be placed in any part of such structure

which may tend to hinder such fish. In case the enclosure, where the fish are
taken, is furnished with a board floor, an opening extending from the floor five
feet towards the top of the weir or trap must be equivalent to extending the
said opening from bottom to top. Any violation of this section, is punishable
as prescribed in section 1179. Informers are entitled to one-half of all fines.
—[Chap. 96, Code 1881.

WALLA AND KITTITAS COUNTIES.—Every person who shall, within the counties of Walla Walla and Kittitas, for any purpose, take, kill, injure, or destroy, have in possession, sell or offer for sale, any **Prairie Chicken**, **Sage Hen**,
Grouse, **Pheasant**, or **Quail** between the 1st day of December and the 15th day of
October next ensuing; or any **Blue Mountain Grouse** between the 1st day of December and the 1st day of August next ensuing, is guilty of a misdemeanor.
—[Laws 1888.

Fish Nets, Etc.—§ 1. It is unlawful to build or cause to be built, or to place or
cause to be placed any *Fish Trap, Net, Weir, Seine, or Net* in any fresh water
stream or creek in Washington Territory that will reach more than two-thirds
the way across such stream or creek, or that will wholly prevent the passage of fish
either up or down such stream or creek....§ 2. It is unlawful to use or cause to
be used any fish trap, weir, seine, or net in any of the lakes of this Territory for
the purpose of catching fish....§ 3. Nor shall it be lawful to use or cause to be
used any *Minerals, Drugs, Fish Berries, or Poison of any kind for the purpose of
catching fish* ... § 4. Nor shall it be lawful to build, or cause to be built, any
Dam or other Obstruction that shall reach wholly across any stream or creek in
said Territory, unless a chute or passage shall be provided sufficient to allow
fish to pass either up or down such stream or creek....§ 5. Any person violating any of the provisions of either of the foregoing sections is liable to a penalty
of $25 for each offense. *It is lawful for any person to remove or destroy any trap,
seine, or net found in use in any stream, creek, or lake in Washington Territory, in
violation of this act.*—[Laws 1871.

Game and Fish Laws of Wyoming.

§ 1. It is unlawful to kill, hunt, or pursue any **Deer, Elk, Moose, Mountain
Sheep, Mountain Goat, Antelope,** or **Buffalo**, save only from the 1st day of September and the 1st day of December, inclusive, in each year, or kill or catch, by
means of any pitfalls or traps, any of the above named animals at any time.
No non-resident of this Territory shall pursue, hunt, or kill any deer, elk, moose,
mountain sheep, mountain goat, antelope, or buffalo by any means whatever;
provided, that from the 1st day of October to the 1st day of January, inclusive, the actual and *bona fide* residents of this Territory may pursue, hunt, or
kill said animals, but not by means of any pitfall or trap; but no more than
two of any of said animals shall be killed in any one day; and having in possession more than two of said animals killed in any one day is *prima facie*
evidence of a violation of this act.....§ 2. It is unlawful to kill or destroy by
any means, any **Ruffed Grouse**, save only from the 15th day of August to the 15th
day of October in each year.....§ 3. It is unlawful to destroy by any means,
any **Colon** or **Quail** until the 1st day of September 1891, and thereafter only during the month of September in each year; or to kill any Ptarmigan, **Pinnated
Grouse, Sharp-Tailed Grouse, Sage Grouse, Red Grouse,** or any other grouse or sage
hen, save only from the 1st day of August to the 15th day of November, inclusive, in each year, or to kill in any one day more than ten of any of the game
birds herein before mentioned. Having in possession in any one day more
than thirty-five of any of the game birds mentioned in this section is *prima
facie* evidence of such violation.-....§ 5. It is unlawful to kill any Wild Duck,
Brant, or **Goose** from the 1st day of May to the 15th day of August in any year;
or (§ 6) to sell, or expose for sale, the carcase or any part thereof suitable for
food of any of the kinds or species of animals or birds protected by this act,
save during the open season provided by this act, and for thirty days next succeeding the time limited for the killing of such animals and birds; provided,
it is lawful to sell any colon or quail for the purpose of breeding, or the taking
of the same alive for preservation through the winter. It is also lawful for any
person to take alive on his own premises at any time and in any manner any of

the animals or birds hereinbefore mentioned for the sole purpose of domesti-cating, or for scientific or breeding purposes....§ 7. It is unlawful to obtain by barter any green or untanned hide or hides of any of the animals men-tioned in section one of this act, or for any corporation, company, person or persons, to Transport or have in possession for transportation any green or un-tanned hide or hides of the animals mentioned in section one of this act after the expiration of sixty days from the passage of this act; but none of the pro-visions of this section shall apply to hides in transit through this Territory from other States or Territories...§ 8. It is unlawful for any railroad company, express company or Common Carrier, or any of their agents or employees or other person or persons to receive or have in their possession for transportation any carcasses or parts of carcasses of any of the birds or animals named in this act, or to transport the same after the expiration of ten days next succeeding the time limited for the killing of such birds or animals; but none of the provisions of this section shall apply to game in transit through this Territory from other States or Territories....§ 9. It is unlawful to kill more of the animals named in section one than can be Used or disposed of for food; but nothing in this act shall deprive any citizen of this Territory from killing any game for the use of himself or family for food, if killed within ten miles of the residence of such citizen....§ 10. Any corporation, company, person or persons violating any of the provisions of this act shall be deemed guilty of a misdemeanor, and on conviction shall be subject to a fine of $100 for each offense, or imprisonment not more than ninety days, or both....§ 11. Any person giving information of any violation of this act to the prosecuting attorney or any justice of the peace of the county in which such violation occurred, shall be entitled to one-half of all such fines recovered....§ 12. Chapter 59, laws 1839, and all acts and parts of acts in conflict herewith, are repealed.—[Chap. —, laws 1882.

www.ingramcontent.com/pod-product-compliance
Lightning Source LLC
Chambersburg PA
CBHW021551270326
41930CB00008B/1456